MW00509095

THE ULTIMATE NFT GUIDE

Secure Your Investment with NFT, A simple Guide to Crypto NFT

Jeanette D. Schmidt

Copyright © 2022 by Jeanette D. Schmidt

All rights reserved.

No portion of this book may be reproduced in any form without written permission from the publisher or author, except as permitted by U.S. copyright law.

Contents

INTRODUCTION

They are ubiquitous, although many people are unaware of their existence. After amassing a global collection of art and gaming via multimillion-dollar auctions, NFT has established a following among celebrities and companies.

Adidas developed some in collaboration with the Bored Ape Yacht Club and then collaborated with Prada on the NFT project. McDonald's and Coca Cola, for example, have used NFT into their marketing strategies. If you are still completely perplexed, which we do not blame you for being.

What are NFTs? will be discussed in detail below. Additionally, we'll explain how creative professionals may make advantage of them.

Whether you believe it is a passing trend or a significant new alternative for musicians, there is no disputing that the NFTs are producing all songs and that at least one advertising has united them.

Therefore, what are non-ferrous transition metals (NFTs)? Continue reading to understand how NFTs function, how they are manufactured, and why they are so contentious.

Once you've gained momentum, you're ready to continue studying our NFT world series of topics. We've written articles highlighting the greatest NFT artwork and the best NFT cryptocurrency for advertising. If you decide to construct your own NFT, be sure to check out our instructions to making and selling NFTs, as well as our recommended NFT marketplaces. Additionally, you'll want to ensure that you're working with the greatest possible digital software.

CHAPTER # 1

WHAT ARE NFTS AND HOW ARE THEY TO BE USED?

NFT is an acronym for non-fungible token, which means that concealed within this original illustration is a single unit of non-tradable data stored on a digital ledger that makes use of blockchain technology to establish proof of ownership. This is essentially the same or a similar technology to that used by cryptocurrencies such as Bitcoin and Ether.

Ether is used to ensure the uniqueness of each NFT; however, who is proving this?

Unlike a bitcoin, however, each NFT is unique, and thus cannot be transacted in the same way. The file contains additional data that elevates it above the realm of pure currency and places it in the realm of, well, anything. As a result, the NFT has been elevated to the status of a collectible digital asset, just as physical artwork must be valued. Any digital file type that is easily reproducible can be stored as NFT to uniquely identify the original copy. The NFTs that you are more likely to have seen or read about are typically stunning future works of art. NFTs can be created from any type of file image, art, music, or video previously. Even tweets and memes undergo NFT conversions. Almost anything unique that can be stored digitally and has value can be made into NFTs.

They function similarly to any other collectible item, such as a painting or a drawing classic action, except that instead of purchasing the actual item, you pay a file and equal to, rather than providing proof that you own the original copy.

Anything that is capable of being converted to digital is a possible NFT. Everything from your drawings, photos, videos, GIFs, music, video game items, selfies, and even a tweet can be converted to NFT, which enables you to provide live translation online using cryptocurrencies.

However, what distinguishes NFTs from other digital forms is their use of Blockchain technology. For those who are unfamiliar with Blockchain, it is a decentralized ledger in which all transactions are recorded.

COMMISSIONS FROM THE NFTS

Are you an artist? Do you have a job where you'd like to earn money? Increase your earnings by selling your work through NFT. As an NFT, you can create or produce and sell digital content.

Including original digital artworks, music, memes, and audio-video clips.

A New Yorker once sold his farts under the moniker NFT! Thus, continue; your imagination is your only constraint.

TRADE OF NFTS

You can invest in NFTs by purchasing them and profitably selling them in less than six months! NFTs, on the other hand, are not all created equal. Some are worth millions of dollars, while others are worthless. As a collector, you must examine the coin critically to determine its future resale value.

GAMING NFT NFT

We live in an exciting era in which anyone can play for a chance to win. The Blockchain-based games allow you to purchase and trade in-game items using NFTs. These are now popular collectibles, similar to how Crypto Kitties are used in the game. Over $300,000 has been raised in a single crypto chat. With the more affordable NFT, there are more games available than in recent years. Some players even give their collection away to newcomers.

NFTS Gambling

What Exactly is a Bet? Staking, in the context of cryptocurrency, refers to the process of storing digital assets as "stakes" and allocating them to individuals willing to operate them. In exchange, they distributed rewards to you. You can wager your NFT on various websites, including Rplanet, to win prizes and offers. INVEST IN NFT START-UPS

Investing in startups is another way to earn indirectly with non-fungible tokens. If there is one thing that the NFTs have established, it is that they are not a passing crypto trend.

Numerous promising NFT startups demonstrate unique innovations in the cryptocurrency space. It would be wonderful to invest in them as they embark on the path toward a revolutionary future.

As the big brands continue to grow in popularity, they become increasingly popular. While exchange collection and NFT generation are hot topics in the current game, they will have more options in the future.

As is the case with any other investment, there is risk involved. Bear in mind that in order to monetize them, you must conduct thorough research and invest prudently.

CHAPTER # 2

NEXT GENERATION TELEPHONE SYSTEMS AND BLOCKCHAIN

The Blockchain era is arguably the most overhyped development of the twenty-first century. Originally developed to support bitcoin, Blockchain now powers a slew of other cryptocurrencies, and developers are working to integrate the technology into industries such as medicine, art, and finance.

It may be beneficial to understand how blockchain operates, why it is expensive, and what distinguishes it from other network technologies.

A blockchain is defined as a decentralized, immutable ledger that enables the recording and monitoring of transactions and assets within an enterprise community.

Facts underpin business. The sooner it is obtained and corrected, the better. Blockchain technology is well-suited for encrypting those data points. It enables immediate, shared, and unalterable facts to be stored on an immutable ledger and accessed only with the permission of community contributors. A Blockchain community can keep track of orders, payments, accounts, and manufacturing processes, amongst other things. And, because the contributor's percentage is a transparent representation of the truth, you can see the entire history of a transaction, providing you with increased confidence as well as new efficiencies and opportunities.

Bear in mind that a blockchain is a collection of software programs that functions as a decentralized ledger distributed among the nodes of a communication network. What sets it apart from other online databases or purchasing and selling systems is its immutability: we will exchange virtual possessions peer to peer. Without the approval of the majority of the community, no one can regulate or reverse a transaction. That is a significant advantage when it comes to using the Internet.

At one end of the virtual asset spectrum are cryptocurrencies such as bitcoin, which are used in payment networks such as the Bitcoin blockchain. Bitcoins are fungible, which means that each bitcoin is identical in terms of price and characteristics to all other bitcoins. Thus, if you have a bitcoin agreement, you may update one bitcoin with each other without violating the contract's terms.

NFTs are at the opposite end of the spectrum: each token represents a unique cost. NFTs encompass a variety of unique items—they are no longer limited to collectibles but also include delivery and death certificates, property deeds, and the identities of Internet of Things devices. You couldn't update an Andrew Wyeth portrait with Mike Winkelmann's artwork and expect no one to notice, under an agreement.

While the bubble surrounding Crypto Kitties—the one-of-a-kind NFT phenomenon—may have deflated as well, the excitement surrounding the public sale of Beeple's paintings demonstrated the potential of NFTs. It is a cost-effective venture limited only by your imagination, your technical capacity to create it, and the marketing, accounting, and legal assistance necessary to carry it out.

HOW ARE BLOCKCHAIN AND NFT DIFFERENT?

What is electronic foreign exchange trading?

Digital forex refers to the digital representation of foreign currency and payments stored in a virtual wallet. By withdrawing coins from a financial institution or ATM, a person can convert virtual forex to coins.

While digital currency does not have a physical counterpart in the real world, it shares many of the same characteristics as traditional currency. A person can acquire, switch, or substitute virtual currency for any other currency. A man or woman can pay for goods and services with virtual currency. Digital forex transactions can be made between any two points on the globe.

A significant financial institution virtual currency (CBDC) is a centralized virtual currency that is managed and monitored by a significant financial institution in the United States. A CBDC makes use of a virtual token or digital document to represent the digital form of US fiat currency. Although no major financial institution-sponsored virtual currency has been officially launched in the United States, a number of significant banks, including a group of state-owned banks in China, have released pilot programs and research projects to determine the viability of CBDCs. The Federal Reserve Bank of the United States is also considering expanding its virtual currency reserves.

Virtual forex structures come in the following configurations:

A virtual forex device backed by a central financial institution Stablecoins, or cryptocurrency with a fixed price,

Bitcoin and other unstabilized cryptocurrencies

What distinctions exist between non-fungible tokens, cryptocurrencies, and virtual currencies?

NFTs, cryptocurrencies, and virtual currencies all have their own distinct characteristics.

Contrary to virtual currencies and cryptocurrencies, NFTs cannot be traded or exchanged. Each NFT is unique, distinguishing it from fungible tokens, such as virtual currency and cryptocurrency, which can be freely sold or exchanged.

Because digital currencies are centralized, they may be regulated by a combination of human beings and computer systems. On the other hand, cryptocurrencies and NFTs are decentralized, with the regulations set by the largest group within each.

Additionally, virtual currency is not widely used. For instance, a man or woman cannot pick the deal with the wallets and observe each cash switch because this information is confidential. However, the existence of cryptocurrencies and NFTs is obvious. Because each transaction is stored in a public blockchain community, any person can view the transactions of any other person.

As is the case with cryptocurrency, including Bitcoin, a CBDC is entirely data-driven and would not exist in the real world. Unlike cryptocurrency and NFTs, CBDCs are backed by governments, which means they are much more likely to be recognized as legitimate forms of payment. Digital coins are a form of virtual currency that is backed by a large financial institution.

HOW IS BLOCKCHAIN COMPUTER TECHNOLOGY APPROPRIATE?

Using bitcoin as an example, the following describes how Blockchain — also known as distributed ledger technology — works:

Bitcoin transactions are entered and transmitted through a network of highly effective computer systems known as nodes.

This network of numerous nodes distributed throughout the sector competes to validate the transaction using laptop algorithms. Bitcoin is awarded to the miner who first completes a new block. These rewards are funded through a combination of newly minted bitcoin and community fees that are directly surpassed by the client and seller. Bitcoin mining is the term used for this.

Once the transaction is cryptographically confirmed, the sale is recorded in a block on the distributed ledger. The deal must then be secured by the majority of networks.

By utilizing a cryptographic fingerprint known as a hash, blocks are permanently linked to all previous blocks of bitcoin transactions, and transactions are processed.

In a thesis, he discusses "the design of a distributed computing system capable of being established, maintained, and trusted by mutually suspicious groups." However, it was a 2008 paper titled "Bitcoin: A Peer to Peer Electronic Cash System" written under the pseudonym Satoshi Nakamoto that brought academic theory to life. What type of money is electronic? Cryptocurrency is a decentralized payment system that operates independently of a bank. It is a peer-to-peer payment system that enables anyone to send and receive payments from anywhere in the world. Rather than being transported and exchanged for physical currency in the real world, cryptocurrency payments exist solely as digital entries in an online database describing specific transactions.

When cryptocurrency is transferred, the transaction is recorded on a public ledger. In virtual wallets, cryptocurrencies are stored. The term "cryptocurrency" comes from the fact that transactions are verified using encryption. Encryption is designed to ensure privacy and security. This refers to the advanced encryption techniques used to secure the storage and transmission of cryptocurrency data between wallets and public ledgers.

Bitcoin, founded in 2009 and still the most well-known cryptocurrency today, was the first cryptocurrency. Trading for profit is a significant concern for cryptocurrencies, with speculators occasionally driving prices sky-high.

Chapter # 3

A Summary of NFTS's History

WHAT SITUATIONS RESULTED IN THE CREATION OF NFTS

Tokens that are not fungible are just one-of-a-kind digital assets. Bitcoin and other fungible assets are. In other words, all Bitcoins are interchangeable and identical. A piece of art is an illustration of a non-fungible token. I may have two digital artworks that are identical in appearance, yet each is distinct.

NFTS was created when and by whom?

Anil Dash and Kevin McCoy pioneered the concept of Non-Fungible Tokens (NFTs) in order to enable artists to market their digital works. (NFTs are unique data structures that may be associated with media such as video or photos.) However, NFTs are already selling cryptocurrency-rich memes for an unthinkable $1 billion. It serves as the market's bedrock. Brooke inquires about the unforeseen repercussions of Dash's innovation in this section. Among these are the enormous environmental costs associated with NFTs, not to mention their potential for covert financing and money laundering without discovery. Dash is also considering enforcing accountability from inside the cryptocurrency community. "Technology is something you can accomplish," Dash asserts. "It can do anything you want, you can still be sorry for it, and it can cope with the consequences."

Non-Fungible Tokens (NFTs) are a sort of digital asset that enables the ownership of a variety of unique and intangible goods, ranging from collectible sports cards to virtual real estate and even digital shoes. Typically, the token itself indicates the file's location and defines how art or audio snippets operate.

One of the primary benefits of digital collectors over physical collectors of items such as Pokemon cards or rare coins is that each communication is unique from the others. This entails the birth and spread of the fake collector, since each item can be traced back to the original issuer.

In contrast to conventional cryptocurrencies, NFTs cannot be swapped immediately. This is because no two NFTs are identical, even those belonging to the same platform, game, or collection. Consider it a ticket to a festival. Each ticket carries unique information about the purchaser, such as his or her name, the event's date, and location.

HISTORY IN ITS FIRST FIVE YEARS

Cryptoartic Categories were established in response to cultural occurrences such as CryptoPunks, Rare PEPE, and Cryptositis. These "artists" have been known to acquire these works in exchange for viral network effects and a significant sum of money.

COLOR COINS, 2012-2013

This journey encompasses a diverse cast of characters, artists, and endeavors. NFT's concept was originally dubbed "color coin" and debuted in 2012 at Bitchina. Although the basic concept was simple, it made advantage of the Bitcoin blockchain to store digital collectibles, coupons, investments, and business shares, among other things. They were referred to as emerging technologies that represented an untapped possibility from an use standpoint.

CONTRACTOR YESTERDAY, JANUARY 14TH, 2014

Counterparty was established in 2014 by Robert Dermody, Adam Krellenstein, and Evan Wagner. It is an open-source, decentralized internet protocol and peer-to-peer financial network based on the Bitcoin blockchain. Counterparty operated a decentralized exchange that enabled the production of assets and let users to construct their own transferable money. He was brimming with ideas and prospects, notably the ease with which he traded memes with fakes.

2015: ORDER OF CONTRACTOR

Counterparty teamed up with the Spells of Genesis development team in April 2015. Spells of Genesis' author is a pioneer in transferring game assets to the blockchain using Counterparty and making an initial coin offering. To support the development of Counterparty, the founders developed their in-game money, Bit Crystal.

FOR CONTRACTORS IN 2016: CARD EXCHANGE

A new tendency started to emerge around August 2016. Counterparty has partnered with the famous card game Force of Will to create Counterparty cards. It placed fourth in North American card game sales behind Pokémon, Yu-Gi-Oh, and Magic Force of Will. Entering an ecosystem with no previous knowledge of blockchain or cryptocurrency demonstrates the benefit of storing such assets on a blockchain.

CONTRACTORS RECEIVE RARE PREFERENCE IN 2016

Memes made their blockchain debut in 2016. Memes began to circulate on Counterparty networks in October 2016. Individuals started adorning particular memes dubbed "Rare Pepes" with valuables. Rare Pepes is a meme featuring an intriguing frog mascot that has developed a large following over time. Originally a cartoon figure called Pepe Frog, it has grown to become one of the most famous memes on the internet, causing a constant phenomenon. Rare Pepes began selling as Ethereum gained popularity in early 2017. Portion creator Jason Rosenstein co-hosted the first live Rare Pepe auction at the inaugural Rare Digital Art Festival with Louis Parker. CryptoArt was founded on the Rare Pepe Wallet, and this is the first time that producers from all around the globe may submit and sell their work. It was the first time that digital art could be considered valuable in and of itself. Cryptopunk is a term that describes the year 2017.

As trading in Rare Pepes increased in popularity, Larva Labs co-founders John Watkinson and Matt Hall produced a unique Ethereum character. There are no two identical characters, and the maximum number is 10,000. Cryptopunk is a reference to the 1990s Bitcoin experiment and is a cross between ERC721 and ERC20. ERC20, the most widely used Ethereum token standard, has rules that let tokens to interact but is incompatible with the creation of unique tokens. Here comes ERC721, the Ethereum blockchain standard for non-fungible tokens. ERC721 enables the tracking of individual tickets' ownership and movement inside a single smart contract. NFT 2021 Explosive

NFTs sparked renewed attention in 2021. Other locks, like as Cardano, Solan, Tezos, and Flow, have started experimenting with the NFTS version in order to create a new standard and ensure that the digital assets offered are genuine. Purchasing surgery in the early 2/4Q of this year 2021, in particular, was astounding.

The frenzy token's origins are significantly more complicated than most people realize. As we go from the experimental to the mainstream age, the future becomes much more possible. Despite the phenomenal development we've seen lately, I feel this field is still in its infancy and will continue to flourish. The NFT community will continue to grow in recognition of the influence that NFT can have on the majority of us today. Coins Discuss Coins in detail.

Color Coin might be considered to be the first NFT. Color coins are composed of minuscule units of Bitcoin and may be as little as a satoshi, Bitcoin's smallest unit. Color coins may be used to symbolize a variety of assets, as shown by the following:

Capability to offer encryption for your property The topic of business collaboration

Subscribe Token availability

Collectibles in Digital Format

Demonstrated a significant leap in terms of Bitcoins' potential. However, if everyone agrees on their beliefs, their disadvantages might all reflect the same thing. Because the Bitcoin scenario language did not attempt to include this sort of behavior, it became as powerful as the color coins as a weak player. For instance, three individuals represent 100 nonferrous coins, which correspond to 100 weeks. Even a single participant will bring the system to a halt if we do not have colored coins reflecting the company's equity. The first reference to non-ferrous coins seems to be in early 2012 blog posts titled "Bitcoin 2 dubbed Bitcoin 2. X (AKA Color Bitcoins) - Initial Characteristics." He believes that a bitcoin is not a collection of assets or a use of a collection of assets or use cases, but rather a bitcoin that is a component of a " Genesis Transaction ". In a typical Bitcoin transaction, you may be identifiable and distinctive.

By December 4, 2012, the potential value of this new item had not been evaluated. "There will be another document in a few months in 2013," according to a December 4, 2012, statement. It was titled "Colorful COINS - BITCOINX". Coins are obviously painted. The system performs optimally in the permitted environment, however it does sometimes make use of the database. Nonetheless, the color coins paved the way for future research and preserved the majority of the NFT's foundations. The enormous opportunity to invest in the deployed book's real work is recognized.

HOW ABOUT SOME INTRIGUING NFTs?

According to Google Trends, the most popular NFT artworks between January and September 2021 were as follows:

For $2.9 million, the first tweet was sold. Hash mark, which was auctioned for sixteen million dollars $4 million price tag for Doge NFT For $6 million, Grimes NFT was sold.

Everyday: For $69 million, the first 5,000 days were sold. The NFT of Rick and Morty was sold for $1.6 million. For $6.6 million, Crossroad NFT was sold. CryptoPunks #7804 fetched $7.5 million at auction. Genesis Estate NFT, $1,500,000

The source code for the World Wide Web's non-functional testing (NFT) protocol was sold for $5.4 million.

TWEET ORIGINALE

In March 2006, Twitter co-founder Jack Dorsey sent his first tweet, which read, "I've just setup my Twitter." Sina Estavi, a Malaysian customer who paid with cryptocurrency ether, bought the tweet. Dorsey used the tweet to raise $2.9 million for charity.

HASH MARKS

Hash marks are a vibrant collection of artworks created by more than 70 artists from around the world. It features 16,384 one-of-a-kind digital portraits—one of the coins sold for a profit of 100,000 percent in three days.

NFT DOGNE

The original 2010 meme, dubbed 'Doge,' was inspired by the infamous Shiba Inu dog Kabosu, who inspired the development of the dogecoin cryptocurrency. PleasrDAO is the collective that purchased the NFT and is now selling fractional ownership, which means that anyone can own a dollar's worth of the NFT.

TNF GRIMME

Grimes released a ten-part series, the most popular of which was a one-off video titled "Death of the Old," which featured a cherry, a crucifix, a sword, and glowing lights set to Grimes' soundtrack. Two additional plays, titled "Earth" and "Mars," each with a print run of thousands of copies, each sold for $7,500, with nearly 700 copies sold prior to sales closing.

EACH DAY: THE ORIGINAL 5000 DAYS

Mike Winkelmann's (Beeple's) digital art work. Everyday: Vignesh Sundaresan (a pseudonym for MetaKovan), a Singaporean programmer, purchased The First 5000 Days, a 5000-image collage. In the Metaverse, the artwork is displayed in its entirety in a digital museum.

MORTY AND RICK

Justin Roiland, co-creator of Rick and Morty, recently auctioned off the "Best I Can Do" collection through the NFT

Nifty Gateway auction house. The NFT's commissions were donated to Los Angeles' homeless shelters.

CROSSROADS CROSSROADS CROSSROADS CROSSROA

The crossroads was created in response to the 2020 presidential election and consisted of two sections, one dedicated to Trump's success and failure and the other to his failure. Crossroads was created by Beeple (Mike Winkelmann's) and raised $6.6 million through an auction on the Nifty Gateway.

7804 CRYPTOPUNKS

This CryptoPunk is one of a series of aliens, the rarest of word games. Shalom Mackenzie, the primary investor in DraftKings and Ethereum, acquired NFT (ETH).

GENERATION OF NFT REAL ESTATE

Infinite axie

Sold Genesis land in the heart of the Lunacia world, a critical component of Axie Infinity's gameplay. Danny (Flying Falcon) is a seller, an NFT collector, and a member of the Hashmasks and Cryptopunk communities.

CODE FOR THE NFT GLOBAL WEBSITE

Sotheby's auctioned off the source code for the World Wide Web created by inventor Tim Berners-Lee. Since 1989, when the World Wide Web was launched, NFT has represented ownership of digital goods.

WHO ARE THE MOST PROMINENT USERS OF NFT?

Beeple, aka Mike Winkelmann, is one of the most popular New Forms artists working today. Among his works is a now-famous NFT collage titled Everyday: the First 5000 Days, which sold for an astounding $69 million. The work was created over a 13-year period and includes 5,000 digital images that took a year to create and post. Nothing has sparked more interest in brand marketing in the last year than the NFT (non-fungible token). Since Christie's launched the first digital NFT auction (JPG by Beeple aka Mike Winkelmann sold for $69.3 million), brands have been experimenting digitally with the Metaverse to determine how they can participate in the NFT pie.

NFTs are designed as uncopyable digital assets, similar to owning an original work of art online. They are created using blockchain technology, which means they have a defined security token with a unique name.

While some brands create NFT collections or limited editions to diversify their revenue streams, build brand loyalty, or raise money for a good cause, others do not. Other brands employ them to bolster an image, tell a story, or reach out to new audiences. Additionally, there are additional ways to sell tickets for live events.

And, while they gained prominence last year, they are expected to become mainstream in 2022, establishing themselves as a significant player in the trillion-dollar marketing industry and earning industry recognition. Marketers are increasingly utilizing it to create one-of-a-kind brand experiences, increase brand awareness, and foster engagement.

Brands leverage NFT in novel ways to market new products, commemorate significant events or anniversaries, increase social media followings, support a campaign, or demonstrate support for a charity or movement.

ASICSONE

Asics launched their summer collection in July.

Asics' Sunrise Red collection, one of the first sportswear brands to enter the NFT race, featured limited edition digital sneakers (each of the gallery's nine silhouettes) designed in collaboration with various digital artists. The sports brand describes the initiative as a "celebration of sport and the first step toward a future where digital assets inspire physical activity." Proceeds from 189 digital properties (20 digital assets per silhouette) will be reinvested in artists via Asics digital assets. Program for Artist Residency. Metallic gold was also released as a limited-edition color.

CLINIQUE

Clinique unveiled MetaOptimist, the first limited-edition NFT kit from the Estée Lauder Companies. The global beauty brand held a contest to award three NFTs to Smart Rewards members who shared stories of happiness, hope, and optimism on social media using the hashtags #MetaOptimist #Clinique #Concours. Additionally, instead of the auction system prevalent in NFTs, the winners receive free products.

BELLA TACOS

The NFT's series of events honors the iconic Taco by fusing the digital and physical worlds. Upon purchase of the original "Transforming Taco," participants will receive a $500 e-gift card to spend however they wish. Taco Bell auctioned off 25 NFT GIFs on the NFT Marketplace, Rarible, in order to increase brand awareness while also benefiting a good cause. While each GIF began at a price of US$1, the 25 NFTs sold out in less than 30 minutes and ranged in price from thousands of dollars to US$3,646 each. The proceeds benefit Live Mas scholarship programs that aid in the education of at-risk youth.

MATTEL COLD WHEEL

Mattel, the world's largest toy company, began rolling out NFT across its entire line of collectible Hot Wheels brands in November, releasing 40 different models of Hot Wheels NFTs to consumers at a starting price of US$15 each. There are four- or ten-packs of NFTs featuring the brand's iconic cartoon designs. Each collector has a 5% chance of obtaining a one-of-a-kind token and owning a genuine mint vehicle—economical and limited edition.

COCA COCA COCA

Coca-Cola has released a series of four NFTs to commemorate International Friendship Day on July 30. The NFTs are one-of-a-kind animated digital artworks that provide a multi-sensory experience - when purchased, they reveal unexpected items. The first owner was created to raise expectations and increase entertainment value; surprises include the Decentraland virtual reality platform's wearable "Coca-Cola Bubble Jacket" and the Decentraland virtual reality platform's "Coca-Cola Friendship Card." Among others, contemporary works from the 1960s to the 1940s. The winning bidder also received a fully stocked Coca-Cola fridge, which was auctioned for 72 hours as a one-time "loot box." The NFT auction generated a total of $575,883 for Special Olympics International. Coca-Cola then released a brand new set of four NFTs in December 2021, a carnival-themed collectible digital snowball collection featuring snowfall and polar bears carrying polar bears. As part of the blind box offer, Coke's iconic status conceals the collectible/rare item you've acquired until you complete your purchase.

MCDONALD'S

McDonald's has launched its first-ever NFT promotion to commemorate the return of its limited McRib collection to the fast-food restaurant's menu in November. The world's largest restaurant chain has released a limited number of NFTs (dubbed the MCNFT) as part of a virtual collectible art collection featuring McRibs in order to generate excitement about the restaurant's temporary return. The product's scarcity. The group of ten individual NFT McRibs is only available to those who retweeted the brand's invitation, which over 21,000 people did in just a few hours and nearly 93,000 people did in early 2022. That is an excellent reference point.

PENGUIN IN ITS ORIGINAL FORM

To engage its younger audience, Original Penguin partnered with TikTok influencer artists to create and deliver its first-ever NFT auction in November. For the first time ever, a fashion brand has commissioned TikTok videos as the primary NFT asset. Eight augmented reality-enabled NFTs were auctioned, three created by the brand and five by TikTok influencers, with interested buyers able to view the NFTs in augmented reality (i.e., walking along a beach lined with virtual penguins) before committing. All proceeds benefited Free Arts NYC, a not-for-profit organization dedicated to assisting youth through art and mentoring programs.

NFL

The NFL announced in November that fans may be eligible for complimentary virtual ceremonial tickets as part of a limited-edition NFT. Fans who attended select games between

Thanksgiving and the end of the 2021 season were eligible to receive an NFT ticket, which could then be traded or sold.

GUCCI

Gucci, the Italian fashion house, took to the digital runway in June, when it auctioned off a newly minted NFT inspired by its Fall/Winter 2021 collection via an online auction hosted by Christie's.

Christie's describes the NFT as a "dream-like landscape with effervescent energy." It is based on Aria, a four-minute film created to accompany a runway show and formatted as a three-channel video playing on loop. The week-long auction concluded with a final sale of US$25,000, with the proceeds benefiting United Nations International Children's Emergency Fund USA's COVAX initiative.

Chapter Two

NEXT GENERATION TELEPHONE SYSTEMS AND BLOCKCHAIN

The Blockchain era is arguably the most overhyped development of the twenty-first century. Originally developed to support bitcoin, Blockchain now powers a slew of other cryptocurrencies, and developers are working to integrate the technology into industries such as medicine, art, and finance.

It may be beneficial to understand how blockchain operates, why it is expensive, and what distinguishes it from other network technologies.

A blockchain is defined as a decentralized, immutable ledger that enables the recording and monitoring of transactions and assets within an enterprise community.

Facts underpin business. The sooner it is obtained and corrected, the better. Blockchain technology is well-suited for encrypting those data points. It enables immediate, shared, and unalterable facts to be stored on an immutable ledger and accessed only with the permission of community contributors. A Blockchain community can keep track of orders, payments, accounts, and manufacturing processes, amongst other things. And, because the contributor's percentage is a transparent representation of the truth, you can see the entire history of a transaction, providing you with increased confidence as well as new efficiencies and opportunities.

Bear in mind that a blockchain is a collection of software programs that functions as a decentralized ledger distributed among the nodes of a communication network. What sets it apart from other online databases or purchasing and selling systems is its immutability: we will exchange virtual possessions peer to peer. Without the approval of the majority of the community, no one can regulate or reverse a transaction. That is a significant advantage when it comes to using the Internet.

At one end of the virtual asset spectrum are cryptocurrencies such as bitcoin, which are used in payment networks such as the Bitcoin blockchain. Bitcoins are fungible, which means that each bitcoin is identical in terms of price and characteristics to all other bitcoins. Thus, if you have a bitcoin agreement, you may update one bitcoin with each other without violating the contract's terms.

NFTs are at the opposite end of the spectrum: each token represents a unique cost. NFTs encompass a variety of unique items—they are no longer limited to collectibles but also include delivery and death certificates, property deeds, and the identities of Internet of Things devices. You couldn't update an Andrew Wyeth portrait with Mike Winkelmann's artwork and expect no one to notice, under an agreement.

While the bubble surrounding Crypto Kitties—the one-of-a-kind NFT phenomenon—may have deflated as well, the excitement surrounding the public sale of Beeple's paintings demonstrated the potential of NFTs. It is a cost-effective venture limited only by your imagination, your technical capacity to create it, and the marketing, accounting, and legal assistance necessary to carry it out.

HOW ARE BLOCKCHAIN AND NFT DIFFERENT?

What is electronic foreign exchange trading?

Digital forex refers to the digital representation of foreign currency and payments stored in a virtual wallet. By withdrawing coins from a financial institution or ATM, a person can convert virtual forex to coins.

While digital currency does not have a physical counterpart in the real world, it shares many of the same characteristics as traditional currency. A person can acquire, switch, or substitute virtual currency for any other currency. A man or woman can pay for goods and services with virtual currency.

Digital forex transactions can be made between any two points on the globe.

A significant financial institution virtual currency (CBDC) is a centralized virtual currency that is managed and monitored by a significant financial institution in the United States. A CBDC makes use of a virtual token or digital document to represent the digital form of US fiat currency. Although no major financial institution-sponsored virtual currency has been officially launched in the United States, a number of significant banks, including a group of state-owned banks in China, have released pilot programs and research projects to determine the viability of CBDCs. The Federal Reserve Bank of the United States is also considering expanding its virtual currency reserves.

Virtual forex structures come in the following configurations:

A virtual forex device backed by a central financial institution Stablecoins, or cryptocurrency with a fixed price,

Bitcoin and other unstabilized cryptocurrencies

What distinctions exist between non-fungible tokens, cryptocurrencies, and virtual currencies?

NFTs, cryptocurrencies, and virtual currencies all have their own distinct characteristics.

Contrary to virtual currencies and cryptocurrencies, NFTs cannot be traded or exchanged. Each NFT is unique, distinguishing it from fungible tokens, such as virtual currency and cryptocurrency, which can be freely sold or exchanged.

Because digital currencies are centralized, they may be regulated by a combination of human beings and computer systems. On the other hand, cryptocurrencies and NFTs are decentralized, with the regulations set by the largest group within each.

Additionally, virtual currency is not widely used. For instance, a man or woman cannot pick the deal with the wallets and observe each cash switch because this information is confidential. However, the existence of cryptocurrencies and NFTs is obvious. Because each transaction is stored in a public blockchain community, any person can view the transactions of any other person.

As is the case with cryptocurrency, including Bitcoin, a CBDC is entirely data-driven and would not exist in the real world. Unlike cryptocurrency and NFTs, CBDCs are backed by governments, which means they are much more likely to be recognized as legitimate forms of payment. Digital coins are a form of virtual currency that is backed by a large financial institution.

HOW IS BLOCKCHAIN COMPUTER TECHNOLOGY APPROPRIATE?

Using bitcoin as an example, the following describes how Blockchain — also known as distributed ledger technology — works:

Bitcoin transactions are entered and transmitted through a network of highly effective computer systems known as nodes.

This network of numerous nodes distributed throughout the sector competes to validate the transaction using laptop algorithms. Bitcoin is awarded to the miner who first completes a new block. These rewards are funded through a combination of newly minted bitcoin and community fees that are directly surpassed by the client and seller. Bitcoin mining is the term used for this.

Once the transaction is cryptographically confirmed, the sale is recorded in a block on the distributed ledger. The deal must then be secured by the majority of networks.

By utilizing a cryptographic fingerprint known as a hash, blocks are permanently linked to all previous blocks of bitcoin transactions, and transactions are processed.

In a thesis, he discusses "the design of a distributed computing system capable of being established, maintained, and trusted by mutually suspicious groups." However, it was a 2008 paper titled "Bitcoin: A Peer to Peer Electronic Cash System" written under the pseudonym Satoshi Nakamoto that brought academic theory to life. What type of money is electronic? Cryptocurrency is a decentralized payment system that operates independently of a bank. It is a peer-to-peer payment system that enables anyone to send and receive payments from anywhere in the world. Rather than being transported and exchanged for physical currency in the real world, cryptocurrency payments exist solely as digital entries in an online database describing specific transactions.

When cryptocurrency is transferred, the transaction is recorded on a public ledger. In virtual wallets, cryptocurrencies are stored. The term "cryptocurrency" comes from the fact that transactions are verified using encryption. Encryption is designed to ensure privacy and security. This refers to the advanced encryption techniques used to secure the storage and transmission of cryptocurrency data between wallets and public ledgers.

Bitcoin, founded in 2009 and still the most well-known cryptocurrency today, was the first cryptocurrency. Trading for profit is a significant concern for cryptocurrencies, with speculators occasionally driving prices sky-high.

Chapter # 3

A Summary of NFTS's History

WHAT SITUATIONS RESULTED IN THE CREATION OF NFTS

Tokens that are not fungible are just one-of-a-kind digital assets. Bitcoin and other fungible assets are. In other words, all Bitcoins are interchangeable and identical. A piece of art is an illustration of a non-fungible token. I may have two digital artworks that are identical in appearance, yet each is distinct.

NFTS was created when and by whom?

Anil Dash and Kevin McCoy pioneered the concept of Non-Fungible Tokens (NFTs) in order to enable artists to market their digital works. (NFTs are unique data structures that may be associated with media such as video or photos.) However, NFTs are already selling cryptocurrency-rich memes for an unthinkable $1 billion. It serves as the market's bedrock. Brooke inquires about the unforeseen repercussions of Dash's innovation in this section. Among these are the enormous environmental costs associated with NFTs, not to mention their potential for covert financing and money laundering without discovery. Dash is also considering enforcing accountability from inside the cryptocurrency community. "Technology is something you can accomplish," Dash asserts. "It can do anything you want, you can still be sorry for it, and it can cope with the consequences."

Non-Fungible Tokens (NFTs) are a sort of digital asset that enables the ownership of a variety of unique and intangible goods, ranging from collectible sports cards to virtual real estate and even digital shoes. Typically, the token itself indicates the file's location and defines how art or audio snippets operate.

One of the primary benefits of digital collectors over physical collectors of items such as Pokemon cards or rare coins is that each communication is unique from the others. This entails the birth and spread of the fake collector, since each item can be traced back to the original issuer.

In contrast to conventional cryptocurrencies, NFTs cannot be swapped immediately. This is because no two NFTs are identical, even those belonging to the same platform, game, or collection. Consider it a ticket to a festival. Each ticket carries unique information about the purchaser, such as his or her name, the event's date, and location.

HISTORY IN ITS FIRST FIVE YEARS

Cryptoartic Categories were established in response to cultural occurrences such as CryptoPunks, Rare PEPE, and Cryptositis. These "artists" have been known to acquire these works in exchange for viral network effects and a significant sum of money.

COLOR COINS, 2012-2013

This journey encompasses a diverse cast of characters, artists, and endeavors. NFT's concept was originally dubbed "color coin" and debuted in 2012 at Bitchina. Although the basic concept was simple, it made advantage of the Bitcoin blockchain to store digital collectibles, coupons, investments, and business shares, among other things. They were referred to as emerging technologies that represented an untapped possibility from an use standpoint.

CONTRACTOR YESTERDAY, JANUARY 14TH, 2014

Counterparty was established in 2014 by Robert Dermody, Adam Krellenstein, and Evan Wagner. It is an open-source, decentralized internet protocol and peer-to-peer financial network based on the Bitcoin blockchain. Counterparty operated a decentralized exchange that enabled the production of assets and let users to construct their own transferable money. He was brimming with ideas and prospects, notably the ease with which he traded memes with fakes.

2015: ORDER OF CONTRACTOR

Counterparty teamed up with the Spells of Genesis development team in April 2015. Spells of Genesis' author is a pioneer in transferring game assets to the blockchain using Counterparty and making an initial coin offering. To support the development of Counterparty, the founders developed their in-game money, Bit Crystal.

FOR CONTRACTORS IN 2016: CARD EXCHANGE

A new tendency started to emerge around August 2016. Counterparty has partnered with the famous card game Force of Will to create Counterparty cards. It placed fourth in North American card game sales behind Pokémon, Yu-Gi-Oh, and Magic Force of Will. Entering an ecosystem with no previous knowledge of blockchain or cryptocurrency demonstrates the benefit of storing such assets on a blockchain.

CONTRACTORS RECEIVE RARE PREFERENCE IN 2016

Memes made their blockchain debut in 2016. Memes began to circulate on Counterparty networks in October 2016. Individuals started adorning particular memes dubbed "Rare Pepes" with valuables. Rare Pepes is a meme featuring an intriguing frog mascot that has developed a large following over time. Originally a cartoon figure called Pepe Frog, it has grown to become one of the most famous memes on the internet, causing a constant phenomenon. Rare Pepes began selling as Ethereum gained popularity in early 2017. Portion creator Jason Rosenstein co-hosted the first live Rare Pepe auction at the inaugural Rare Digital Art Festival with Louis Parker. CryptoArt was founded on the Rare Pepe Wallet, and this is the first time that producers from all around the globe may submit and sell their work. It was the first time that digital art could be considered valuable in and of itself. Cryptopunk is a term that describes the year 2017.

As trading in Rare Pepes increased in popularity, Larva Labs co-founders John Watkinson and Matt Hall produced a unique Ethereum character. There are no two identical characters, and the maximum number is 10,000. Cryptopunk is a reference to the 1990s Bitcoin experiment and is a cross between ERC721 and ERC20. ERC20, the most widely used Ethereum token standard, has rules that let tokens to interact but is incompatible with the creation of unique tokens. Here comes ERC721, the Ethereum blockchain standard for non-fungible tokens. ERC721 enables the tracking of individual tickets' ownership and movement inside a single smart contract. NFT 2021 Explosive

NFTs sparked renewed attention in 2021. Other locks, like as Cardano, Solan, Tezos, and Flow, have started experimenting with the NFTS version in order to create a new standard and ensure that the digital assets offered are genuine. Purchasing surgery in the early 2/4Q of this year 2021, in particular, was astounding.

The frenzy token's origins are significantly more complicated than most people realize. As we go from the experimental to the mainstream age, the future becomes much more possible. Despite the phenomenal development we've seen lately, I feel this field is still in its infancy and will continue to flourish. The NFT community will continue to grow in recognition of the influence that NFT can have on the majority of us today. Coins Discuss Coins in detail.

Color Coin might be considered to be the first NFT. Color coins are composed of minuscule units of Bitcoin and may be as little as a satoshi, Bitcoin's smallest unit. Color coins may be used to symbolize a variety of assets, as shown by the following:

Capability to offer encryption for your property The topic of business collaboration

Subscribe Token availability

Collectibles in Digital Format

Demonstrated a significant leap in terms of Bitcoins' potential. However, if everyone agrees on their beliefs, their disadvantages might all reflect the same thing. Because the Bitcoin scenario language did not attempt to include this sort of behavior, it became as powerful as the color coins as a weak player. For instance, three individuals represent 100 nonferrous coins, which correspond to 100 weeks. Even a single participant will bring the system to a halt if we do not have colored coins reflecting the company's equity. The first reference to non-ferrous coins seems to be in early 2012 blog posts titled "Bitcoin 2 dubbed Bitcoin 2. X (AKA Color Bitcoins) - Initial Characteristics." He believes that a bitcoin is not a collection of assets or a use of a collection of assets or use cases, but rather a bitcoin that is a component of a " Genesis Transaction ". In a typical Bitcoin transaction, you may be identifiable and distinctive.

By December 4, 2012, the potential value of this new item had not been evaluated. "There will be another document in a few months in 2013," according to a December 4, 2012, statement. It was titled "Colorful COINS - BITCOINX". Coins are obviously painted. The system performs optimally in the permitted environment, however it does sometimes make use of the database. Nonetheless, the color coins paved the way for future research and preserved the majority of the NFT's foundations. The enormous opportunity to invest in the deployed book's real work is recognized.

HOW ABOUT SOME INTRIGUING NFTs?

According to Google Trends, the most popular NFT artworks between January and September 2021 were as follows:

For $2.9 million, the first tweet was sold. Hash mark, which was auctioned for sixteen million dollars $4 million price tag for Doge NFT For $6 million, Grimes NFT was sold.

Everyday: For $69 million, the first 5,000 days were sold. The NFT of Rick and Morty was sold for $1.6 million. For $6.6 million, Crossroad NFT was sold. CryptoPunks #7804 fetched $7.5 million at auction. Genesis Estate NFT, $1,500,000

The source code for the World Wide Web's non-functional testing (NFT) protocol was sold for $5.4 million.

TWEET ORIGINALE

In March 2006, Twitter co-founder Jack Dorsey sent his first tweet, which read, "I've just setup my Twitter." Sina Estavi, a Malaysian customer who paid with cryptocurrency ether, bought the tweet. Dorsey used the tweet to raise $2.9 million for charity.

HASH MARKS

Hash marks are a vibrant collection of artworks created by more than 70 artists from around the world. It features 16,384 one-of-a-kind digital portraits—one of the coins sold for a profit of 100,000 percent in three days.

NFT DOGNE

The original 2010 meme, dubbed 'Doge,' was inspired by the infamous Shiba Inu dog Kabosu, who inspired the development of the dogecoin cryptocurrency. PleasrDAO is the collective that purchased the NFT and is now selling fractional ownership, which means that anyone can own a dollar's worth of the NFT.

TNF GRIMME

Grimes released a ten-part series, the most popular of which was a one-off video titled "Death of the Old," which featured a cherry, a crucifix, a sword, and glowing lights set to Grimes' soundtrack. Two additional plays, titled "Earth" and "Mars," each with a print run of thousands of copies, each sold for $7,500, with nearly 700 copies sold prior to sales closing.

EACH DAY: THE ORIGINAL 5000 DAYS

Mike Winkelmann's (Beeple's) digital art work. Everyday: Vignesh Sundaresan (a pseudonym for MetaKovan), a Singaporean programmer, purchased The First 5000 Days, a 5000-image collage. In the Metaverse, the artwork is displayed in its entirety in a digital museum.

MORTY AND RICK

Justin Roiland, co-creator of Rick and Morty, recently auctioned off the "Best I Can Do" collection through the NFT Nifty Gateway auction house. The NFT's commissions were donated to Los Angeles' homeless shelters.

CROSSROADS CROSSROADS CROSSROADS CROSSROA

The crossroads was created in response to the 2020 presidential election and consisted of two sections, one dedicated to Trump's success and failure and the other to his failure. Crossroads was created by Beeple (Mike Winkelmann's) and raised $6.6 million through an auction on the Nifty Gateway.

7804 CRYPTOPUNKS

This CryptoPunk is one of a series of aliens, the rarest of word games. Shalom Mackenzie, the primary investor in DraftKings and Ethereum, acquired NFT (ETH).

GENERATION OF NFT REAL ESTATE

Infinite axie

Sold Genesis land in the heart of the Lunacia world, a critical component of Axie Infinity's gameplay. Danny (Flying Falcon) is a seller, an NFT collector, and a member of the Hashmasks and Cryptopunk communities.

CODE FOR THE NFT GLOBAL WEBSITE

Sotheby's auctioned off the source code for the World Wide Web created by inventor Tim Berners-Lee. Since 1989, when the World Wide Web was launched, NFT has represented ownership of digital goods.

WHO ARE THE MOST PROMINENT USERS OF NFT?

Beeple, aka Mike Winkelmann, is one of the most popular New Forms artists working today. Among his works is a now-famous NFT collage titled Everyday: the First 5000 Days, which sold for an astounding $69 million. The work was created over a 13-year period and includes 5,000 digital images that took a year to create and post. Nothing has sparked more interest in brand marketing in the last year than the NFT (non-fungible token). Since Christie's launched the first digital NFT auction (JPG by Beeple aka Mike Winkelmann sold for $69.3 million), brands have been experimenting digitally with the Metaverse to determine how they can participate in the NFT pie.

NFTs are designed as uncopyable digital assets, similar to owning an original work of art online. They are created using blockchain technology, which means they have a defined security token with a unique name.

While some brands create NFT collections or limited editions to diversify their revenue streams, build brand loyalty, or raise money for a good cause, others do not. Other brands employ them to bolster an image, tell a story, or reach out to new audiences. Additionally, there are additional ways to sell tickets for live events.

And, while they gained prominence last year, they are expected to become mainstream in 2022, establishing themselves as a significant player in the trillion-dollar marketing industry and earning industry recognition. Marketers are increasingly utilizing it to create one-of-a-kind brand experiences, increase brand awareness, and foster engagement.

Brands leverage NFT in novel ways to market new products, commemorate significant events or anniversaries, increase social media followings, support a campaign, or demonstrate support for a charity or movement.

ASICSONE

Asics launched their summer collection in July.

Asics' Sunrise Red collection, one of the first sportswear brands to enter the NFT race, featured limited edition digital sneakers (each of the gallery's nine silhouettes) designed in collaboration with various digital artists. The sports brand describes the initiative as a "celebration of sport and the first step toward a future where digital assets inspire physical activity." Proceeds from 189 digital properties (20 digital assets per silhouette) will be reinvested in artists via Asics digital assets. Program for Artist Residency. Metallic gold was also released as a limited-edition color.

CLINIQUE

Clinique unveiled MetaOptimist, the first limited-edition NFT kit from the Estée Lauder Companies. The global beauty brand held a contest to award three NFTs to Smart Rewards members who shared stories of happiness, hope, and optimism on social media using the hashtags #MetaOptimist #Clinique #Concours. Additionally, instead of the auction system prevalent in NFTs, the winners receive free products.

BELLA TACOS

The NFT's series of events honors the iconic Taco by fusing the digital and physical worlds. Upon purchase of the original "Transforming Taco," participants will receive a $500 e-gift card to spend however they wish. Taco Bell auctioned off 25 NFT GIFs on the NFT Marketplace, Rarible, in order to increase brand awareness while also benefiting a good cause. While each GIF began at a price of US$1, the 25 NFTs sold out in less than 30 minutes and ranged in price from thousands of dollars to US$3,646 each. The proceeds benefit Live Mas scholarship programs that aid in the education of at-risk youth.

MATTEL COLD WHEEL

Mattel, the world's largest toy company, began rolling out NFT across its entire line of collectible Hot Wheels brands in November, releasing 40 different models of Hot Wheels NFTs to consumers at a starting price of US$15 each. There are four- or ten-packs of NFTs featuring the brand's iconic cartoon designs. Each collector has a 5% chance of obtaining a one-of-a-kind token and owning a genuine mint vehicle—economical and limited edition.

COCA COCA COCA

Coca-Cola has released a series of four NFTs to commemorate International Friendship Day on July 30. The NFTs are one-of-a-kind animated digital artworks that provide a multi-sensory experience - when purchased, they reveal unexpected items. The first owner was created to raise expectations and increase entertainment value; surprises include the Decentraland virtual reality platform's wearable "Coca-Cola Bubble Jacket" and the Decentraland virtual reality platform's "Coca-Cola Friendship Card." Among others, contemporary works from the 1960s to the 1940s. The winning bidder also received a fully stocked Coca-Cola fridge, which was auctioned for 72 hours as a one-time "loot box." The NFT auction generated a total of $575,883 for Special Olympics

International. Coca-Cola then released a brand new set of four NFTs in December 2021, a carnival-themed collectible digital snowball collection featuring snowfall and polar bears carrying polar bears. As part of the blind box offer, Coke's iconic status conceals the collectible/rare item you've acquired until you complete your purchase.

MCDONALD'S

McDonald's has launched its first-ever NFT promotion to commemorate the return of its limited McRib collection to the fast-food restaurant's menu in November. The world's largest restaurant chain has released a limited number of NFTs (dubbed the MCNFT) as part of a virtual collectible art collection featuring McRibs in order to generate excitement about the restaurant's temporary return. The product's scarcity. The group of ten individual NFT McRibs is only available to those who retweeted the brand's invitation, which over 21,000 people did in just a few hours and nearly 93,000 people did in early 2022. That is an excellent reference point.

PENGUIN IN ITS ORIGINAL FORM

To engage its younger audience, Original Penguin partnered with TikTok influencer artists to create and deliver its first-ever NFT auction in November. For the first time ever, a fashion brand has commissioned TikTok videos as the primary NFT asset. Eight augmented reality-enabled NFTs were auctioned, three created by the brand and five by TikTok influencers, with interested buyers able to view the NFTs in augmented reality (i.e., walking along a beach lined with virtual penguins) before committing. All proceeds benefited Free Arts NYC, a not-for-profit organization dedicated to assisting youth through art and mentoring programs.

NFL

The NFL announced in November that fans may be eligible for complimentary virtual ceremonial tickets as part of a limited-edition NFT. Fans who attended select games between Thanksgiving and the end of the 2021 season were eligible to receive an NFT ticket, which could then be traded or sold.

GUCCI

Gucci, the Italian fashion house, took to the digital runway in June, when it auctioned off a newly minted NFT inspired by its Fall/Winter 2021 collection via an online auction hosted by Christie's.

Christie's describes the NFT as a "dream-like landscape with effervescent energy." It is based on Aria, a four-minute film created to accompany a runway show and formatted as a three-channel video playing on loop. The week-long auction concluded with a final sale of US$25,000, with the proceeds benefiting United Nations International Children's Emergency Fund USA's COVAX initiative.

NFTS CAN BE USED FOR THE FOLLOWING PURPOSES

IMPROVE CREATORS' EARNINGS

Today, NFTs are most frequently used in the field of virtual content. This is because business is broken in the modern era. The systems eat away at content creators' earnings and earning potential.

A social media platform that sells commercials to the artist's followers earns money when an artist publishes artwork on the platform. They receive publicity in exchange, but advertising does not cover expenses.

NFTs power a new author economic system in which creators retain control of their work and do not surrender it to the methods used to promote it. Ownership is ingrained in the content. When they advertise their content, the budget is quickly depleted. If the new owner sells the NFT, the original author may also receive royalty payments on a consistent basis. This is guaranteed on each occasion the token is offered, as the writer's deal is embedded in the token's metadata – which cannot be modified.

IMPROVE THE POTENTIAL FOR GAMING

Sport builders have numerous visible hobbies with NFTs. NFTs can provide ownership data for in-game objects, thereby enhancing in-game economies and providing numerous benefits to players.

You can purchase objects to use in a variety of everyday video games. You might even earn money if the object gained in popularity. However, if the item becomes an NFT, you can recoup your investment by selling it once the game is completed.

For game developers – as NFT issuers – this could mean earning a royalty on each time an object is re-offered to the open market. This results in an even more incredible mutually beneficial business model in which gamers and developers profit from the secondary NFT market.

This other method ensures that even if a game is not maintained by the developers, the items you've accumulated remain yours.

Eventually, the items you grind for in-sport will outlast the video games. Even if you do not maintain a sport, you will always have control over your possessions. This is how sports memorabilia and feature fees become virtual memorabilia outside of the sport.

Additionally, Decentraland, a digital reality game, enables you to purchase NFTs representing digital parcels of land that you can use as your place of residence.

IMPROVE REMARKABILITY OF ETHEREUM ADDRESSES

The Ethereum Name Service utilizes NFTs to provide an easier-to-remember name for your Ethereum transaction, such as my wallets. You can then request that someone send you ETH via my wallet. in comparison to 0x123456789......

This works in conjunction with a website area call, resulting in an IP transaction.

This works in conjunction with a website area call, enhancing the fantastic memories associated with an IP transaction. And, as with domain names, ENS names are subject to a fee, which is typically determined entirely by the duration and relevance of the name. You do not want a site registry to facilitate the transfer of ownership to ENS. Alternatively, you can use an NFT marketplace to trade your ENS names.

RECEIVE CRYPTOCOIN AND ADDITIONAL NFTS

Indicate the location of a decentralized internet website, such as Ethereum.eth. Continue reading for more information on decentralizing your website. Keep any type of record, including profile information such as e-mail addresses and Twitter handles.

MATTER OF FACTORY MANUFACTURING

Physical objects have not evolved as far as their virtual counterparts in terms of tokenization. However, numerous projects are investigating the tokenization of real estate, one-of-a-kind style objects, and more.

As NFTs are deeds, you may someday use ETH to purchase a car or a house and receive the act as an NFT in exchange (within the same transaction), as things become more high-tech. It is no longer difficult to imagine a world in which your Ethereum wallets become the most important item in your automobile or home – your door is unlocked via cryptographic evidence possession.

You can use NFTs as collateral for decentralized loans with precious property such as motors and assets represented on Ethereum. This is especially advantageous if you have ceased to be wealthy in coins or cryptocurrency but still own physical objects for a fee.

NOTIFICATION OF NFTS AND DEFICUMENTATION OF DEFICUTION

The NFT and DeFi worlds are beginning to collaborate in a variety of exciting ways.

LOANS BACKED BY THE NATIONAL FINANCIAL TRADING CENTER

DeFi packages enable you to borrow money using collateral as security. For instance, you pledge ten ETH as collateral for a loan of five thousand DAI (a stable coin). This ensures that the lender is compensated – if the borrower fails to repay the DAI, the lender receives the collateral. However, now that everyone has access to high-quality cryptocurrency, anyone can use it as collateral.

Increasingly, projects are recognizing the value of using non-fungible tokens as collateral. Consider acquiring another extraordinary CryptoPunk NFT in a day – they can fetch hundreds of dollars at current prices. By pledging this as collateral, you may be able to obtain the right of entry into a mortgage that follows the same set of rules. If you fail to pay the DAI on a subsequent payment, your CryptoPunk may be assigned as collateral to the lender. This might work with something you tokenize as an NFT at some point.

And this is not a difficult task for Ethereum, as each world (NFT and Defi) has an equal infrastructure proportion.

PROPERTY OWNERSHIP ON A PROPORTIONAL BASIS

Additionally, creators of NFTs have the option of creating "shares" for their work. It enables investors and enthusiasts to purchase a portion of an NFT without purchasing the entire thing. It expands the opportunities available to both NFT minters and creditors.

Fractionalized NFTs can now be traded on decentralized exchanges (DEXs) such as Uniswap, which are no longer restricted to NFT marketplaces. Increased consumers and sellers in this manner.

The typical fee for an NFT can be expressed in terms of the fractional price of its fractions.

You have a better chance of owning and utilizing items that are important to you. Being priced out of proudly owning NFTs is more difficult.

While this remains experimental, you can learn more about fractional NFT ownership at the following exchanges:

NFTX

This, in theory, will open up the possibility of owning a small Picasso. You could become a shareholder in a Picasso NFT, giving you a say in matters such as revenue sharing. It is possible that someday, quickly proudly owning a fragment of an NFT will automatically enroll you in a decentralized self-sufficient organization (DAO) responsible for the asset's management.

CHAPTER # 5

HOW DO NFTS WORK?

These Ethereum-powered institutions enable strangers, such as overseas shareholders of an asset, to collaborate safely without always needing to trust various individuals.

As previously said, this is a growing market. NFTs, DAOs, and fractionalized tokens all continue to expand at varying rates. However, their whole infrastructure exists and they can collaborate without difficulty since they all talk in the same language: Ethereum. Therefore, keep an eye on this location.

PROOF OF OWNERSHIP IF YOU ARE THE OWNER OF AN NFT

Possessing an NFT is not synonymous with proudly possessing the thing it symbolizes. When you buy an NFT, you get a token that is registered on a blockchain, a distributed database of transactions. While this token is unique, it normally attempts to be an easily reproduced asset. The customer of an NBA Top Shot Moment, an NFT that symbolizes an NBA highlight clip, owns the NFT: they may exchange, sell, or give away their individual token. However, purchasers cannot prevent others from seeing highlight footage, many of which are available on YouTube. The NFT understands that its possessor has the right to do anything; for example, in the case of a video clip, the proprietor may also have the right to download or stream it. The amount of rights issued may be decided by the NFT's minter. However, a right to get access to or observe something is very separate from proudly holding rights to the depicted object. NFT utilizes Blockchain technology because it provides clients with exclusive ownership of a virtual asset. For instance, if you are a cartoonist and convert your virtual investment to an NFT, what you get is proof of ownership, facilitated by the use of Blockchain technology.

In simple terms, when you list your NFT on the market, you pay a gas cost (transaction fee) for the use of the Blockchain, and your virtual artwork is then registered on the Blockchain, indicating that you (your handle) own the particular NFT. This grants you entire ownership—which cannot be updated or altered by anybody, even the market proprietor.

As a result, an NFT is formed, or as crypto enthusiasts refer to it, "minted," in order to get certain ownership rights. NFTs will have the most basic ownership structure, with just one proprietor at a time. Apart from physical ownership, NFT owners may also digitally sign their artworks and maintain extensive records of their NFTs' information. This is most easily observable to the one who sold the NFT.

NFTs differ from ERC-20 tokens such as DAI or LINK in that each token is unique and not necessarily divisible. NFTs enable the assignment or declaration of ownership of a particular piece of virtual data, which can be traced using Ethereum's Blockchain as a public record. To show virtual or non-virtual assets, an NFT is coined from virtual objects. For instance, an NFT may want to represent the following:

Art in the Digital Age

GIFs

Collectables

Music\sVideos

Items from the Real World

Title to a vehicle

Admission to a genuine international event

Invoices that have been tokenized

Documents juridiques

Signatures

Numerous other possibilities with which to experiment! An NFT may only have one owner at a time. Ownership is determined by the uniqueID and metadata, neither of which can be replicated by any token. NFTs are created using devious contracts that assign ownership and alter the NFTs' transferability. When someone generates or mints an NFT, they execute code stored in intelligent contracts that adhere to proprietary standards, such as ERC-721. These data are added to the Blockchain, which is used to regulate the NFT. From a high level, the minting process consists of the following steps:

Adding a new block

Statistical validation

Statistic recording on the Blockchain

Each minted token is identified by a unique identifier. This is inextricably linked to at least one Ethereum transaction.

They are no longer immediately interchangeable 1:1 with other tokens. For instance, 1 ETH is equivalent to any other ETH. This is not true for NFTs.

Each token has a proprietor, who is easily verifiable.

They are Ethereum-based and may be purchased and traded in an Ethereum-based NFT marketplace. In other words, if you customize an NFT, you may easily demonstrate a one-of-a-kind one.

Showing you own an NFT is quite similar to proving you have ETH in your account.

For instance, suppose you purchase an NFT and the token is transmitted to your wallets using your public address.

The token verifies the authenticity of your replication of the virtual document. Your own secret serves as proof of possession of the genuine.

Another technique to demonstrate your private the NFT is to use signed messages to demonstrate your private the unique key at the back of the handle.

As mentioned before, your unique secret serves as proof of possession of the genuine. This indicates that the back's unique keys are capable of altering the NFT.

A signed message may be used to demonstrate that you customise your keys without disclosing them to everyone, so demonstrating that you are also unique to the NFT!

It is not manageable in any way.

ROYALTIES

Each time your NFT work is sold on a commercial marketplace, you earn a portion of the selling price. NFT royalty payments are infinite and are handled automatically by smart contracts. Most commercial marketplaces let you to choose your royalty rate; 5-10% is considered a normal royalty.

Certain NFTs will frequently pay royalties to their creators while being acquired. The original owners of Euler Beats Originals gain an 8% royalty on each purchase of the NFT. Additionally, a few sites, such as Foundation and Zora, assist their artists with income. This is still a developing concept; yet, it is maximal power.

This is automated, allowing authors to take a seat, return, and receive royalties when their artwork is purchased by other characters. Identifying royalties may be difficult and inaccurate, which means that many artists do not earn the commission they deserve. If your NFT includes a royalty, you will never distribute it.

CHAPTER 6

WHAT IS FUNGIBILITY?

The term "fungible asset" refers to an asset whose components are interchangeable, which means they may be indistinguishable. In other words, asset elegance is fungible, meaning that each unit of the asset has the same market value and validity. For instance, a pound of 24-karat gold, regardless of its shape, is identical to another pound of 24-karat gold. Commodities, fiat currencies, bonds, precious metals, and cryptocurrencies are all additional examples of fungible asset instructions.

However, an identical transaction involving a fungible asset does not always imply the replacement of identical devices. As long as the transaction occurs between identical units of the same type and with the same percentage of functionality, it can be considered an identical transaction. For example, a five-dollar invoice may be exchanged for five one-dollar payments; both are valid. The American dollar is the fungible asset in this instance, while the payments represent its underlying value.

By and large, the fungibility property is applied to the maximum number of cryptocurrencies. For instance, we should not overlook the fact that Bitcoin is fungible, which means that each unit of BTC is equivalent to another, implying that they share the same first-class and functionality. Therefore, it makes no difference where Bitcoin blocks are issued (mined); all Bitcoin devices are connected to the same blockchain and have the same functionality. It's worth noting that if someone forks the blockchain and creates a new Bitcoin, the currency will not be considered unique because it may be part of another network.

As a result of BTC and similar cryptocurrencies' inherent traceability, some money is likely to be less appropriate than others - particularly if they were previously used in dubious or illicit activities. Several merchants and service providers may also refuse to accept Bitcoins as bills if they believe the criminals have previously used actual cash.

Contrary to popular belief, this reality does not negate Bitcoin's fungibility characteristics. Fungibility refers to a variety of different concepts, and regardless of their transactional history, all Bitcoins remain identical in terms of quality, technology, and functionality. Similarly, the American dollar is a fungible asset, despite the fact that criminals have abused it for decades. IN CRYPTO, FUNCTIONALITY

Fungible objects or commodities are those that can be exchanged for items of a similar type or with different properties. Foreign currency, for example, is a fungible asset because it can be exchanged for other currencies, goods, or services.

To be fungible, an asset must have a predetermined value and be interchangeable with other objects of comparable value. Bitcoin is considered a fungible asset because its value is quantifiable across currencies and it can be sold and purchased at a fixed price. Additionally, fungible property can be damaged or purchased for infractions, making it easier to trade for similar objects. HOW COME NFTS ARE INVISIBLE TO FUNGUS?

Unlike bitcoin and other cryptocurrencies, NFT is a digital asset that is stored on blockchains (cryptographic virtual ledgers); however, each token is unique.

It's excellent for things like certifying virtual artwork.

The majority of NFTs incorporate virtual paintings via images, videos, GIFs, and music. In theory, a virtual object can be converted to an NFT.

Chapter Four

TYPES OF NFTS

ARTWORKS

Art is the most well-known maximal configuration of NFT. NFTs became an excellent way for artists to advertise their excellent works online, even if they are not physically present. Numerous of the most expensive NFTs on the market are now pieces of art. According to Luna, the most cherished NFT ever created is titled "EVERYDAY'S: THE FIRST 5000 DAYS" and was created in collaboration with renowned artist Beeple. This piece was listed at a staggering $ 69%.

Numerous extraordinary high-priced NFTs are rupturing the financial institutions of billionaires. Additionally, works of video art are included in this category. Short films or even GIFs have been pushed like hotcakes for a million dollars. Notably, a 10-second looping film titled "Crossroad" has offered $6.6 million for a naked Donald Trump laying on the floor. Additionally, with the assistance of Beeple, this one became extra.

ACCESS

According to the description, Access NFTs are a kind of token that allows its owner to access communities, research, or products in both the virtual and physical worlds. In other words, these types of NFTs may be used as access tickets, and their applications span both the virtual and physical realms. In contrast to collectible artwork NFTs, there are currently few instances of contemporary Access NFTs. Early demonstrations and use cases demonstrate that NFT has access to tokens that can take on the look of a standard event price tag. Possession may be easily monitored by issuing verifiably unique tickets through a blockchain. It's unobtrusive to see how fictitious Access NFTs may give access to genuine foreign studies, such as live music performances and meet-and-greets with your favorite influencer.

COLLECTIBLES

Following that, collectibles, the collecting of artwork has grown significantly over the previous many decades. Not long ago, the primary markets were characterized by collectible shops and exchanges.

The majority of collectibles and memorabilia transactions have relocated to the virtual domain, where they found a dependable best friend in NFTs.

NFTs have a straightforward use in the collectibles market. This is often due to collectibles, such as a remarkable Panini soccer trading card with an unmatched price tag, or Jimi Hendrix at Woodstock in 1969. A fine bottle of wine or a cute kitten get their value from their uniqueness and irreplaceability, making them the ideal candidate for NFTs.

Collectibles are high-priced items that collectors may seek for and acquire. Collectors might range from speculators seeking short-term gains to crypto magnates with an eye for the extraordinary. However, the categories do not have to be limited to artwork, music, video clips, sports, or video games.

IN-GAME OBJECTS AND CHARACTERS

Video games represent another frontier in the NFT field. Companies are not presenting whole video games as non-transferable technologies. Rather than that, they may advertise material found inside the recreation, such as skins, characters, and other things. Nowadays, users may purchase tens of thousands of copies of DLC property; yet, an NFT asset may be unique and exclusive to at least one customer.

Developers, on the other hand, may advertise both standard DLC and a limited version of it through the NFT marketplace.

NAME RESTRICTIONS

Domains are the next NFT application after gaming. Since the late 1990s and early 2000s ".com" boom, domains have developed into their own asset class, with a variety of virtual markets devoted to the purchasing and selling of those sometimes valuable commodities.

Despite this, some domain names are fetching tens of thousands of dollars. A pop and its inherent value derive from the fact that area owners may acquire a piece of the internet, build a business around it, grow it, and then sell it for a profit, or so one would hope.

Due to the inherent capabilities of their structures, domains and NFTs no longer share many commonalities; this effectively makes domains and NFTs the appropriate form for non-fungible tokens. Additionally, this may enhance domain names by providing additional proof of ownership characteristics, allowing the holder to access a plethora of additional financial options.

These include storing the space on the blockchain simultaneously to strengthen security measures, simplifying space transfer, and gaining access to the NFT ecosystem's exponentially more liquid secondary markets.

Many corporations are already taking an interest in blockchain-based domains in the same way that venture capitalists and technology traders did. Domain names dating from the early 2000s might be a goldmine of potential revenue. Additionally, this speculative feeling is worsened by ongoing Metaverse developments, which indicate that domain name proprietors may be able to use their domain names as NFTs to establish businesses in the digital realm, such wearable stores or NFT marketplaces. That may be worth considering.

Domain names are not immune to NFT fever spreading. You may register for a site visit and advertise it at the NFT market, which has an added value. Generally, you'll want to hire a third-birthday birthday celebration employer to modify your local phone number. If you acquire one in the NFT market, you will be able to declare exclusive custody of the call, thereby eliminating the middlemen.

MEMES If you're bored with your nft notion, you may buy and trade memes on the NFT market. What's interesting is that in a few instances, the meme's protagonist is actually the vendor. At, you'll find some of the most popular memes, like Nyan Cat, Bad Luck Brian, and Disaster Girl.

THE WEB 2.0'S DATABASES

Today, you may extend NFTs to include data stored in a centralized web2 database using cryptographic approaches and decentralized facts shops.

This may be something straightforward, such as your watching selections, or something more spectacular, such as your whole social network. This enables easy switching between providers and total control over your data, which is a critical component of the web3 vision.

We've witnessed an explosion of invention in the field of NFTs this year. This will very certainly continue to be true for decades, given web3 is still in its infancy.

TICKETS FOR AN EVENT

Additionally, several of the NFT styles may be compatible with event tickets. These types of NFTs enable individuals to attend events such as music galas and musical events in order to validate their identity and access. On a specific blockchain platform, event organizers should mint multiple NFT tickets. Customers should purchase tickets during a public sale and retain them in their wallets for easy access through mobile phones.

IDENTITY

Scarcity is a defining characteristic of non-fungible tokens. Each NFT is unique and cannot be substituted with another. The procedure for recognizing NFTs is identical to that for identifying event tickets. They may act as unique identifiers, assisting identification control systems in a reliable manner.

It is fairly uncommon for certifications and licences to have packages of identification-based NFTs. Minting certificates and licenses, as well as non-fiduciary tokens, for the purpose of establishing and validating a person's facts should replace the identifying control sector. Additionally, identity-based NFTs may instill confidence in individuals that they may retain evidence of their identification on them without fear of losing it. The list, which ranges from $30,000 to $770,000 in value. Currently, the most valuable top meme is the Doge meme, which was purchased for an eye-popping $4 million.

PHOTOGRAPHY

NFTs may be utilized for a variety of purposes; nevertheless, it is the reverse of those tokens that fires the madness. People began to understand that a one-of-a-kind virtual object, similar to a work of art, would command a significant economic price owing to its rarity. They provide artists, buyers, and creditors alike a diverse range of current prospects in contemporary artwork.

The NFT market facilitates transactions between anybody interested in crypto artwork or in art in general. These internet communities enable artists to produce and promote virtual works of art that might otherwise go unnoticed.

In the case of photography, you may tokenize a picture, which means that whomever has the token also owns the exact image. Individuals may check it and photograph it, for instance; yet, the most able owner may exist.

The images in question may remain available on the internet indefinitely, despite being captured and shared by tens of thousands of Internet users (like an easy .jpg picture).

Let us use the case of Vivian Maier as an illustration. Vivian Maier is the photographer and writer of the photos; nevertheless, John Maloof owns the films, which he sold at a public auction. Specifically, each image. It originates from a particular function and occurs in a number of forms, including Kodak Tri-X 8667073. Each image is unique on a roll, which means that if you possess Alternatively, if you expand image variety 5, it will stand in stark contrast to image variety 6. Each roll of film, each photograph, is distinct from the others. Its dimensions are singular. Vivian Maier's artworks, on the other hand, are accessible to the public through exhibitions, publications, and online instruction. John Maloof's proprietorship, on the other hand, remains.

By enabling creators to place a digital signature on their virtual works, NFTs act as a certificate of authenticity, as a piece sold in the form of an NFT cannot be counterfeited. For photographers, each photograph will take on a life of its own, similar to a series of images devoted to a particular film role. However, if the photographer is the creator, the purchaser of the NFT becomes the owner of the paintings, which he or she may resell as desired. A virtual photograph or a print from a film can be duplicated; however, if it is not a limited/numbered edition or, more specifically, the NFT, it can acquire significant value.

Another exciting feature that this device enables is the connection of royalty agreements to photographers' non-disclosure agreements. It entitles them to a percentage of the income generated whenever the asset is transferred; in other words, when the NFT is offered to another party.

WHY NFTS AND PHOTOGRAPHY COLLABORATE SO WELL

Nowadays, the majority of photographs are virtual or have been scanned and converted to virtual.

Because photography is almost always in two dimensions, or flat, breeding on monitors is straightforward.

The quality of monitors and equipment used to display images online continues to improve, providing an accurate representation of the work. Simultaneously, as was not the case previously, it became increasingly popular to look at print in order to appreciate a photograph's high degree of satisfaction. The blockchain-based tokenization of artwork is analogous to period versions in photography. It may be open to the public or restricted to a specific group of people. Rare in the physical sense vs. rare in the digital sense As a result, NFTs enable photographers to specify the version of their work that they require, while also allowing the purchaser to know exactly what is available. There is a degree of verifiability. Photographs are a well-known type of artwork. By 2020, the global smartphone market will have grown to 3.5 billion units, and almost everyone will own one. Social media platforms display a plethora of virtual images. As a result, humans are used to viewing images on monitors.

ASSESSMENTS OF ACTUAL VALUE

While there are few examples of NFTs being used as tokens for real-world items, the NFT industry's growth may change that. For instance, numerous NFT projects are devoted to the tokenization of both real and luxurious property. NFTs are deeds, and they may be used to facilitate the acquisition of a vehicle or a domestic. As a result, NFTs representing actual international property can take advantage of the possibilities associated with cryptographic proof of possession.

REDEEMABLE

Unisocks pioneered a novel concept in which a token could be redeemed for a physical good. This procedure is applicable to a large number of offline items.

For instance, many high-end creditors of tangible personal property store their holdings in a vault. You may wish to create a virtual token for them, allowing for digital presentation and trading, reducing friction and intermediaries, and expanding UX possibilities.

SPORTS

The NFT concept has the appearance of a supersuit designed specifically for the sports activities industry. The NBA is fully aware of this: their NBA Top Shot platform has generated $500 million in revenue and over 800,000 customers since its October 2020 beta launch.

NBA Top Shot is a blockchain-based trading card platform that enables basketball fans to buy, sell, and trade officially certified video highlights ("moments") featuring their favorite players.

As a league or group, you may choose to develop your market in order to facilitate the distribution of your sports club's unique series of NFT cards. Alternatively, you could create an online game in which NFT cardholders compete against each other in digital tournaments.

If athletes wish to create collectible sports cards, they can set up a custom image graph consultation and region unique photographs. Another possibility is that they would struggle to play cards depicting their career highlights. Each playing card must feature an original image and be distinct.

CARDS FOR SHIPPING

NFTs engaged in the purchase and sale of playing cards are digital representations of the underlying physical asset. By virtue of their representation on the blockchain, those playing cards gain immutability and public ownership verification. Even if the physical model is lost or destroyed, the NFT will bear and remain attached to the blockchain for the duration of its existence.

Individuals can develop a digital representation of those playing cards by creating a token on Ethereum or another smart contract blockchain. These non-fungible tokens contain information about the card, most notably the image. These can be stored, viewed, and transferred via a wallet that supports NFT.

Humans can create, acquire, and promote those objects via a variety of systems. OpenSea and Hoard are two of the most prominent at the moment.

Trading cards, like artwork, are unique objects whose entry into the virtual realm is accelerating at the same rate that collectibles as a whole are gaining a funding class.

Apart from cryptocurrency, income from buying and selling credit cards was exploding.

As previously stated, VIRTUAL WORLDS Fungible Tokens (FTs) are a significant factor in enhancing the excitement and profitability of the digital era. A non-fungible token (NFT) is a type of cryptographic asset that demonstrates the holder's ownership of a particular object. It could be music, a sporting asset, a work of virtual art, or real estate, among other things. This also applies to the real estate ecosystem. This innovation's critical feature is that it cannot be used in place of Fungible. As such, an NFT is a specific type of transaction. Due to its rarity, its uniqueness. Additionally, each NFT's underlying metadata distinguishes it from others of its kind and makes it unique to its owner. NFT is a representation of digital factors in the digital universe, including lands. As of early 2021, the expenses associated with digital lands will equal those associated with physical property.

Numerous examples demonstrate the disruptive and innovative nature of NFTs and the digital world. Axie Infinity recently purchased digital land for 1.5 million dollars in the ether. This demonstrates the collaborative nature of each innovation's disruptive potential.

They are represented by avatars and can interact with other users, play games, build houses, and acquire art, among other things.

Virtual reality (VR) and virtual gaming often coexist. These industries have existed for decades, with gamers spending tens of thousands of dollars each year on firearms and other items for their adventures.

Chapter Five

BENEFITS OF NFTS

CAPABILITY OF RESELLING

The majority of people are concerned with NFTs because they have the potential to generate cash. There are numerous ways for individuals to earn money by reselling them. Investing in NFTs for the purpose of reselling them can result in substantial profits. Some of those collectibles were resold for more than 20,000 USD, while the authentic buyer invested only a few dollars. They resold and made 15,000 USD in a single trade!

ORIGINALITY AND OWNERSHIP

At its heart, an NFT is a device that utilizes Blockchain technology to create non-fungible virtual assets. Two primary blessings may be derived from those characteristics. NFT is primarily responsible for certifying possession. With Blockchain-based NFT, the control report is protected against modifications or changes. As a result, a virtual asset can only have a single legitimate owner at a time. As a result, clients no longer have to worry about counterfeiting.

Then there's authenticity. Through the use of NFT, the virtual object will be transformed into a non-fungible asset that contains unique records. With those specific records, the proprietor's belongings can be maintained in their fee and privilege. Additionally, immutable Blockchain protects NFTs from alteration, deletion, or substitution, allowing NFTs to demonstrate authenticity as a prized quality.

COLLECTIBLES

All NFTs are technically collectibles. They are the unique and most convenient of all that can exist. You may maintain them directly after purchasing them, and their fee will increase over time.

MARKETPLACE THAT IS DECENTRALIZED

NFTs enable creators to earn money immediately from their work. A notable example is an art form in which an artist requires an agent to promote and market their work. NFTs obviate the need for intermediaries, allowing artists or authentic creators to interact and transact directly with their customers. Similarly, this version benefits the creators by charging a fee for each time the NFT is exchanged. SECURE ACCESS TO DATA THROUGH BLOCKCHAIN TECHNOLOGY

When it comes to NFTs, you can be assured of security. Blockchains are inherently decentralized. As a result, the records they maintain are stored in specific nodes distributed throughout the world. At each node, the same database report is constantly available. Even if the community is down, there will always be a report of it.

The NFT generation ensures that nodes are always running, regardless of what happens in the Blockchain itself. As a result, nothing can occur to the records. This is not the most advantageous due to the amount of money they earn, but due to their specific amounts. It's obvious that the NFT Blockchain generation has a plethora of advantages, which makes it extremely profitable. They no longer merely provide superior benefits to creators and resellers. There is considerable potential for NFTs to become a critical component of the future of the majority of industries.

ROYALTIES

To summarize, non-fungible tokens (NFT) are indisputablely beneficial to clients. While NFT requires additional information regarding its applicability, cyber security, and exploitation, its miles have been demonstrated to be a viable exercise in a variety of industries in the future.

TRANSFERABILITY

The purchase and sale of NFTs is entirely based on clever contracts. A creative agreement is self-sufficient, secure, precise, and impervious to interruption. The use of an innovative deal facilitates the transfer of ownership of NFT because it most directly requires the fulfillment of specific conditions between purchaser and dealer in accordance with its outline.

Numerous games offer in-game items, which gamers can purchase to enhance their gaming experience. On the other hand, in-game gadgets are restricted to the game's environment, and players cannot use them elsewhere. Additionally, if the sport loses popularity, game enthusiasts may lose money on in-recreation souvenirs or items.

In the case of NFTs, game developers may create them for in-game items for which players may wish to withhold their virtual wallets. Additionally, players can utilize in-recreational activities outside of the sport or promote them to earn money.

Because NFTs are based on intelligent contracts, they simplify the process of transferring ownership. Smart contracts define unique requirements for the purchaser and dealer to meet before possession transfers can be completed.

INCREMENT THE RATE AT WHICH INCLUSIVE GROWTH OCCURS

DLT economies will be closely monitored over the next few years with the assistance of all major funding players, as the benefits of decentralizing finance are too compelling to ignore — decreased transaction friction due to automation, significantly faster (real-time) results and analysis of market conditions, increased protection through transparency, and a higher degree of customization for economic products and services.

Adopting decentralized finance through the use of dominant players could have a beneficial effect on everyone else.

Tokens are the foundation of this new system, and non-fungible tokens are a subset of tokens. Charge tokens behave similarly to money, protection tokens behave similarly to shares, application tokens provide capabilities such as area or bandwidth, and hybrid tokens combine these tokens into new forms. If that sounds a little perplexing and exciting, it is.

The critical takeaway here is that tokens will update not only shares and different investment products, but additionally the entire concept of intermediaries between you and your purchases, whether or not that intermediary is a funding broker, a credit card company, a platform company, or a bank. The decentralized economic system will result in a far more transparent and direct marketplace.CAPABILITY OF RESELLING

The majority of people are concerned with NFTs because they have the potential to generate cash. There are numerous ways for individuals to earn money by reselling them. Investing in NFTs for the purpose of reselling them can result in substantial profits. Some of those collectibles were resold for more than 20,000 USD, while the authentic buyer invested only a few dollars. They resold and made 15,000 USD in a single trade!

ORIGINALITY AND OWNERSHIP

At its heart, an NFT is a device that utilizes Blockchain technology to create non-fungible virtual assets. Two primary blessings may be derived from those characteristics. NFT is primarily responsible for certifying possession. With Blockchain-based NFT, the control report is protected against modifications or changes. As a result, a virtual asset can only have a single legitimate owner at a time. As a result, clients no longer have to worry about counterfeiting.

Then there's authenticity. Through the use of NFT, the virtual object will be transformed into a non-fungible asset that contains unique records. With those specific records, the proprietor's belongings can be maintained in their fee and privilege. Additionally, immutable Blockchain protects NFTs from alteration, deletion, or substitution, allowing NFTs to demonstrate authenticity as a prized quality.

COLLECTIBLES

All NFTs are technically collectibles. They are the unique and most convenient of all that can exist. You may maintain them directly after purchasing them, and their fee will increase over time.

MARKETPLACE THAT IS DECENTRALIZED

NFTs enable creators to earn money immediately from their work. A notable example is an art form in which an artist requires an agent to promote and market their work. NFTs obviate the need for intermediaries, allowing artists or authentic creators to interact and transact directly with their customers. Similarly, this version benefits the creators by charging a fee for each time the NFT is exchanged. SECURE ACCESS TO DATA THROUGH BLOCKCHAIN TECHNOLOGY

When it comes to NFTs, you can be assured of security. Blockchains are inherently decentralized. As a result, the records they maintain are stored in specific nodes distributed throughout the world. At each node, the same database report is constantly available. Even if the community is down, there will always be a report of it.

The NFT generation ensures that nodes are always running, regardless of what happens in the Blockchain itself. As a result, nothing can occur to the records. This is not the most advantageous due to the amount of money they earn, but due to their specific amounts. It's obvious that the NFT Blockchain generation has a plethora of advantages, which makes it extremely profitable. They no longer merely provide superior benefits to creators and resellers. There is considerable potential for NFTs to become a critical component of the future of the majority of industries.

ROYALTIES

To summarize, non-fungible tokens (NFT) are indisputablely beneficial to clients. While NFT requires additional information regarding its applicability, cyber security, and exploitation, its miles have been demonstrated to be a viable exercise in a variety of industries in the future.

TRANSFERABILITY

The purchase and sale of NFTs is entirely based on clever contracts. A creative agreement is self-sufficient, secure, precise, and impervious to interruption. The use of an innovative deal facilitates the transfer of ownership of NFT because it most directly requires the fulfillment of specific conditions between purchaser and dealer in accordance with its outline.

Numerous games offer in-game items, which gamers can purchase to enhance their gaming experience. On the other hand, in-game gadgets are restricted to the game's environment, and players cannot use them elsewhere. Additionally, if the sport loses popularity, game enthusiasts may lose money on in-recreation souvenirs or items.

In the case of NFTs, game developers may create them for in-game items for which players may wish to withhold their virtual wallets. Additionally, players can utilize in-recreational activities outside of the sport or promote them to earn money.

Because NFTs are based on intelligent contracts, they simplify the process of transferring ownership. Smart contracts define unique requirements for the purchaser and dealer to meet before possession transfers can be completed.

INCREMENT THE RATE AT WHICH INCLUSIVE GROWTH OCCURS

DLT economies will be closely monitored over the next few years with the assistance of all major funding players, as the benefits of decentralizing finance are too compelling to ignore — decreased transaction friction due to automation, significantly faster (real-time) results and analysis of market conditions, increased protection through transparency, and a higher degree of customization for economic products and services.

Adopting decentralized finance through the use of dominant players could have a beneficial effect on everyone else.

Tokens are the foundation of this new system, and non-fungible tokens are a subset of tokens. Charge tokens behave similarly to money, protection tokens behave similarly to shares, application tokens provide capabilities such as area or bandwidth, and hybrid tokens combine these tokens into new forms. If that sounds a little perplexing and exciting, it is.

The critical takeaway here is that tokens will update not only shares and different investment products, but additionally the entire concept of intermediaries between you and your purchases, whether or not that intermediary is a funding broker, a credit card company, a platform company, or a bank. The decentralized economic system will result in a far more transparent and direct marketplace.

CHAPTER # 9

BEST NFT MARKETPLACES

OPENSEA

OpenSea is one of the most established and extensively utilized non-financial transaction marketplaces. Additionally, it is one of the largest online retailers of NFT, including artwork, music, photography, and sports collectibles.

Additionally, OpenSea now has a gas-free NFT market with the use of a Cross-Blockchain guide. The market has shifted in favor of the Polygon cryptocurrency in recent months. As a result, you may be able to avoid paying fees while trading. According to OpenSea, this strategy enables artists to "earn their way into cryptocurrency for the first time."

RARIBLE

Is an NFT market intended to promote pieces of artwork and collections that are not connected? It gathers sports, gaming, and media industry professionals, as well as artists launching body of work collections. Rarible is a community-owned company that advocates for decentralized governance. It makes use of the platform's token, RARI, and consumers engage in a limited capacity and have a vote on platform changes.

Rarible has teamed with a few large manufacturers, like Adobe, to stabilize artists' work and develop custom NFTs.

Rarible utilizes the Flow and Tezos blockchains in the same way as Ethereum. When you mint your NFT, you get to choose which token to use, and you can also utilize OpenSea to percentage-search for alternatives. Which Blockchain to choose is a fascinating issue to ponder. Ethereum is the most widely used cryptocurrency for NFT minting, although it has a huge carbon footprint and hefty gas prices. Tezos gas costs are cheap (about $0.50), but they are intended at artists liberating collections. Flow employs a technique known as 'lazy minting'; as a result, creators pay near-zero fees, and it is a 'proof-of-stake' Blockchain, providing miles with a smaller carbon footprint than Ethereum.

NiftyGateway

NiftyGateway is perhaps the most enticing large-cash NFT market. It is here that the world's most expensive NFTs have been offered: Beeple's CROSSROAD and Pak's The Merge, which was sold for US$91.eight million in December 2021 (it remains the world's most expensive NFT at the time of writing).

On Twitter, the site enjoys a fair amount of attention and draws NFTs from Hollywood. However, avoid being put off by this. Nifty Gateway has a number of distinguishing characteristics. To begin, it makes use of 'open versions'; a large number of limited-time versions are generated and made available for a fixed fee. No more NFTs are ever provided after the timer expires. This results in a scarcity of secondary income and a robust market. Second, Nifty enables creditors to shop for non-performing debt instruments (NFTs) using fiat cash (government-issued currency). As a result, users may now pay using credit cards rather than cryptocurrencies. This provides an added level of comfort for new consumers who are unfamiliar with cryptocurrency wallets.

SuperRare

SuperRare imbues the NFT area with an additional gallery sensibility. It is an art-first NFT market that prioritizes creative intent and authenticity above meme-friendly artwork. It apparently accepts less than 1% of applicants, which seems snobbish; yet, if you are generic, you understand that you are among a list of adequately selected and fascinating artworks.

You may not come across SuperRare, which is jam-packed with NFTs from Hollywood stars.

SuperRare is a substantial non-traditional market for critical artwork and artists. The approach enables SuperRare to function as a high-end gallery, which is enhanced by a rule allowing its artists to mint one of each of their originals — there are no Editions here. The parts are very few and, as the name implies, extremely uncommon in this manner.

FOUNDATION

The Foundation operates similarly to an exclusive artist's club to which only a select few are invited; it is a community-curated platform controlled by a select group of artists. Although it has only been running for a year, its founders have made a total $163,263.94. To join the Foundation, you must get an invitation from a contemporary artist, and each artist should have a maximum of one invitation.

The majority of creators are more precise and inventive than those on a few markets.

Placing an NFT on Foundation gets the artist 85% of the value, while secondary revenue rewards the artist 10%. This is a drop in comparison to a few other NFT markets; nonetheless, you may find that NFTs on Foundation are priced more competitively on average and retain their worth.

MAKERSPLACE

Is there any fascinating NFT market for artwork with a high degree of extreme? You'll find artists, galleries, and organizations here that include NFTs into their work, including Damien Hirst, Christie's public auction house, and comic great Robert Liefeld.

On MakersPlace, artists are able to digitally sign their work, which is then stored on the Blockchain. Only a limited number of authentic versions are produced, creating a rising scarcity, and purchasers get entire ownership of the painting - even if the artwork is downloaded and reproduced, it will not be authentic or have the artist's virtual signature.

MINTABLE

In fact, this means you can construct an NFT from almost any kind of virtual file – picture, gif, video, audio file, or text document – and submit it to your platform store. It's really simple to use and requires minimal prior knowledge of NFTs, cryptocurrency wallets, or blockchains. While Mintable is pre-configured to support Ethereum, you can also mint Immutable X for free. Mintable University simplifies living even more by providing accessible video tutorials on how to improve on NFTs.

DECENTRALAND

Decentraland is a technological movement sweeping the world. Developing the thriving in the process of establishing a digital network using the NFT as the technological wrap made a huge difference in the market. Minting digital non-fungible tokens inside Decentraland may be the crypto generation's futuristic strategy, as META worlds continue to garner popularity in a variety of ways.

ORIGINALITY REVEALED

KnownOrigin is a marketplace for non-financial transactions. It specializes in distributing rare and collectible pieces of art via timed-launched events dubbed drops, which let artists to control the amount of copies released. This might result in a supply deficit and a subsequent increase in costs. Artists want to join and must undergo screening, which gives the most exclusivity.

This market mints Ethereum, thus when bidding, you should keep in mind the costs and carbon impact. Additionally, KnownOrigin facilitates partnerships on NFTs and makes a concerted effort to improve network communications and give recommendations for drops and revenue, including making secondary revenue in a separate market clean.

INFINITY OF THE AXIE

The Axie Marketplace is the online game Axie Infinity's online store. Axie are legendary animals that may be purchased and trained, pitting them against the Axis of other players in order to win prizes. Gamers may purchase new Axis, whole regions, and other items on the Axie Marketplace as NFTs for use in the game.

The Ethereum Blockchain is used to create the Axie Infinity coins (Axie Shards). As such, they are available for purchase and sale on a variety of distinct NFT markets, as well as on a few cryptocurrency exchanges, including Coinbase Global.

BAKERYSWAP

BakerySwap is also a full-size NFT market, a sizable market with a circulating supply of more than 195 Million USD; BakerySwap continues to be a stable and acceptable NFT market with the crypto generation for minting an NFT.

ENJIN

Enjin Market's reputation as an excellent NFT market is also well-known in a variety of areas. It may enable the exploration and purchase of Blockchain assets, as well as their sale. More precisely, Enjin Marketplace is the optimal destination for Enjin-based non-financial companies. As of now, it has recorded Enjin currency values on virtual assets totaling about $43.80 million. According to reports, the total number of NFTs liable for such large expenditures is around 2.1 billion.

The Enjin Wallet can aid you in swiftly compiling a list of gaming artifacts and gadgets and purchasing them. Creators may access a 'Projects' page that showcases Enjin-powered Blockchain projects. Sport item collections, network-subsidized collectibles, and gamified praise systems should all be included in the duties. As a consequence, by selecting Enjin Marketplace as your preferred NFT market, you may uncover the finest opportunities.

MYTH MARKET

While there is little to say about Myth Market, it is not an isolated NFT market. Myth Market is a network of flexible and simple-to-obtain access to online marketplaces that supports independent manufacturers of virtual buying and selling cards.

At the moment, Myth Market features several noteworthy features, including GPK.Market, Heroes.Market, Shatner.Market, Pepe.Market, and KOGS.Market.

Each of the featured markets is unique to a particular collectibles emblem—for instance, the GPK. The marketplace facilitates the exchange of Garbage Pail Kids cards. As a result, you can see how Myth Market may have an effect on the destiny scope of NFT.

CHAPTER 10

HOW TO CREATE AND MINT NFT?

SELECTION OF ITEM

Let us begin with the fundamentals.

A non-fungible token (NFT) is a one-of-a-kind virtual object with a single owner. You'll want to determine which specific virtual asset you'll be displaying in an NFT. It could be a custom painting, photograph, piece of music, collectible from an online game, meme, GIF, or even a tweet. This rarity carries an NFT premium. This may take the form of a *.jpg, *.bmp, *.wav, or *.mp4 file. It could be pix-obsessed on an iPhone. The NFT may be anything virtual that you require. It's that simple.

Ascertain that you own the intellectual property rights to the object you intend to incorporate into an NFT. Creating an NFT for a virtual asset about which you have little knowledge should land you in felony trouble.

If you're not sure where to begin, consider developing an NFT loyalty card or promotional code for your customers. Additionally, you can draw inspiration from some NFT artwork concepts.

Concentrate on imparting genuine blessings to your intended audience. Giving individuals who own your NFT access to a premium membership or premium service is an accurate example. Always keep this in mind when deciding which Blockchain protocol to use to create difficulty for your NFT tokens. Numerous Blockchain protocols have unique NFT requirements in addition to market and portfolio matching.

For example, tickets created using Binance Smart Chain may readily available only on platforms that support Binance

Smart Chain assets. As a result, we are unable to sell them on platforms such as OpenSea, which is entirely based on Ethereum.

At the moment, the Ethereum Blockchain is the most frequently used for NFT creation. However, a few options have grown in popularity.

Dapper Labs' Binance Smart Chain Flow-through

Tron\sEOS\sPolkadot\sTezos\sCosmos\sWax

TECHNIQUES UTILIZED IN THE CREATION OF NFT ARTWORK

Growing NFT has become extraordinarily simple, no longer requiring professional knowledge, thanks to a variety of tools. It is worth noting that because NFT is a relatively new and dynamically growing field, it is reasonable to assume that the complete exciting answers have not yet been developed. As a result of this, we've ranked NFT tokens as one of the newest tokenization trends for 2021.

Additionally, the majority of them are curators rather than creators. The creators of digital artwork consider authentic thoughts and themes. And then categorize them as written content, audio, video, artwork, or skills, for example. In both tradition and finance, good artwork is perpetually valuable. For centuries, artworks were unquestionably considered to b excellent investments.

2021 became a watershed year. NFTs have reintroduced vitality to virtual artwork. If you're curious, virtual and NFT paintings are analogous to cryptographic artwork stored on the Blockchain. Artists and creators no longer require technical details, similar to the ERC-721 standard. Or even the mechanism by which non-fungible tokens operate. There are mechanisms in place to enable artists to create virtual works of art and mint them as NFTs. We discuss several of them in greater detail in the following sections.

SKETCHAR

SketchAR is a mobile application for designers and creators that is powered by artificial intelligence. The app allows creators to create and mint their own NFTs. It was founded by Undeterred, a Lithuanian agency based entirely in Vilnius. According to Andrey Drobitko, the app's CEO and Founder, even inexperienced artists can use it. This enables anyone to become an NFT owner of their creations. Artists are no longer interested in acquiring technical knowledge unless it is absolutely necessary.

To begin, you'll want to use the app's canvas to create your ntings. The drawing tool and augmented reality capabilities pp will assist you in embellishing your work. Once the complete, SketchAR will list them on marketplaces gs. After registering, all customers receive awing lessons, courses, and sketches.

FOTOR creators have the option of minting their NFT artworks within the platform ecosystem. Additionally, the platform integrates with key social media platforms. As a result, customers can immediately market their NFT artwork to an international audience of NFT enthusiasts. The platform's support of international photography competitions will increase NFT adoption. Its primary market segment is the semi-expert and expert communities.

NIFTYKIT'S DROP KIT

It is a pay-per-use software platform that enables customers to customize their intelligent contracts. Except for the software development kit, you can also create a separate mint web page if necessary. Additionally, developers can define their own parameters and customize their NFT paintings. The platform is compatible with both the Ethereum and Polygon blockchains.

The venture is currently on hold. Due to the end-user and developer awareness of the experience, all paid members may receive a $9.ninety-nine month-to-month value. As with the team, the clever contracts are optimized to devour gas fee efficiently. Additionally, the platform no longer charges for airdrops. When multiple airdrops occur, the platform has evolved batch minting technology.

The platform no longer charges commissions on secondar' income, but up to 5% of primary income may be charged

MINTABLE

Mintable is a web-primarily based totally platform utilized by virtual artists of all levels. Artists create NFT inventive endeavors in minutes using the platform. Its simplicity is its maximum vital function. Artists can navigate the platform like guiding a social media site. Likewise, it's far as easy to import a photograph of your virtual paintings and click a button to create a clever contract.

Likewise, artists can manipulate the NFT. Mintable additionally affords its market for artists. This guarantees that any novice new to NFTs and virtual artwork can study as rapidly as possible.

ASYNC

Launched in February 2020, Async has numerous functions aside from others. First, Async isn't always open to everyone. It is like a network wherein NFT artists determine who receives to apply the platform.

Second, the network takes an opportunity method to create virtual artwork. As a result, it permits artists to create their ⌐intings in tokenized layers. In this manner, artists can create ⌐hat extrude their appearance. This is a practical function ⌐always on different NFT platforms.

⌐nal artwork marketplace now no longer ⌐condary income proceeds to artists. As a result, the platform has favorable economics. Artists get to maintain 90 percent of the income proceeds on the immediate sale. All secondary income mint 10 percent for artists. This is a function intrinsic to virtual and crypto artwork.

VARIOUS DAILY USE SOFTWARES:

We can also create our NFTs with daily use softwares. Like, Adobe Photoshop, Adobe Illustrator, After effects, Affinity Photo, etc.. If you are designer and know about any of these software or you have basic knowledge about any of these daily use software. Then it is benefit for you. You can design your NFTs by yourself easily. You can design your NFT every single part with these daily use softwares. You can design various parts of your NFT with separate layers and traits.

Traits:

A distinctive quality or characteristic is named as a trait or attribute. Consider yourself as a character. What characteristics cause you to be completely different from others? This brings us to dissecting the character so as to grasp what traits construct the character. Every Small part: eyes, nose, mouth, lips, expressions, headwear, garments that you're sporting, the accessories you carry, all mix to create you look however you are doing. Therefore, these are classified as traits.

SELECTION OF NFT MARKETPLACE

Choosing the proper NFT market should distinguish whether or not your NFT artwork sells or now no longer. It's now no longer pretty much deciding on wherein to promote your artwork primarily based totally on the costs you may pay; you want to recollect which of the numerous NFT marketplaces first-rate fits the sort of NFT you are creating and which Blockchain it uses. Most NFT marketplaces use Ethereum; however, a few choose the inexpensive gas fee (which you need to pay to make your NFT) and higher carbon footprint provided through more modern blockchains.

In the manual below, we have rounded up a number of the first-rate NFT marketplaces on which you could create and promote NFTs (or purchase and acquire them if you are a collector in preference to a creator). Whether you are buying, selling, or simply NFT-curious, the sorts of marketplaces have to fit your needs. After even in case you are no longer making plans to apply to an NFT market at the moment, absolutely everyone within the innovative enterprise will now probably have to recognize what they can be and how they work. If you are nevertheless questioning what an NFT is, then we would advise performing some catching up first by analyzing NFTs?

are up to the mark and suppose NFTs provide a probable your innovative paintings, you will test our manual romote an NFT and our lists of marketplaces to proper NFT crypto on your artwork.

Selection of Blockchain is depends on you, which blockchain you want for your NFT. Some blockchain have gas fees and some blockchain have zero gas fee.

What is Gas Fee?

The gas fee is the unit that measures the quantity of process power needed to perform a group action on the blockchain. Corresponding to the gas you place in your automobile, this gas fuels all specific actions that you just execute on the blockchain.

For every group action or transaction on the Ethereum blockchain, you've got to perform a series of process steps. And every step wants resources to perform. And somebody must procure the utilization of those resources. The miners won't procure these out of their pocket. So, it's the end-users who got to procure the utilization of resources to execute a group action on the blockchain. This fee that you just got to procure the quantity of gas that's used for your group action is understood because of the gas fee.

...ained

B/631

9 781804 766453